SOCIAL EMOTIONAL LEARNING ACTIVITIES FOR KIDS

50+ Practical Activities for Emotional Regulation, Social Skills Building, Self-Management, Critical Thinking, and Decision-Making

FLORIANA S.

TABLE OF CONTENTS

INTRODUCTION TO SOCIAL-EMOTIONAL DYNAMICS!

Social-emotional learning can benefit people of all ages. But students before teenage starts are the best examples of learning the right skills at the right time. SEL can foster more introspection, academic success, and constructive classroom and life conduct in such students who are struggling to make sense of their abilities on the whole.

When looking at academic performance, kids who took part in SEL programs improved their attendance and experienced an 11-percentile rise in their total grades. Students' ability to handle emotional stress, solve issues, and resist negative peer pressure are all positively impacted by the skills taught in social and emotional learning (SEL) programs.

When students are prepared to handle issues that impact them personally, they are more prepared to handle the challenges that adulthood brings. The socio-economic factors are never favorable to all, and such confidence and skills-boosting learnings can provide a much-needed head start to kids who are already being left behind.

Suppose teachers can identify which kids are struggling with social and emotional learning (SEL) concepts. In that case, they may begin to support these students at a younger age, increasing the likelihood that they will acquire these and other beneficial skills at the optimal time. These students can benefit from learning good behaviors that go beyond academic accomplishment. This will help them acquire the "soft skills" needed for many vocations, such as working in a team, understanding people and their behavior, and solving problems. This can ensure that these kids have a good foundation for their academic and future success.

The activities, exercises, and games provided in "Social-Emotional Learning Activities for Kids" will help you lean towards a more interactive class time that sends your students in directions that suit them best. These activities will also help you guide them toward a future that suits them best.

COMPONENT 1

EMOTIONAL REGULATION

Emotional regulation may have been around for a long time, but many kids are unaware of how to express and bear their intense feelings without harming themselves mentally and emotionally.

As teachers, it is our responsibility to flag any emotional disturbances we see in our students. It could be in the form of a bad mood or a sudden need to stay alone and not socialize, among many others.

These emotional fluctuations can be handled by rounding up all students to express their thoughts. It could be by talking, writing, drawing, or simply going over the worksheets that are provided in this section of the book.

Feelings play a big part in shaping us as humans. They let us express how we feel and instigate a reaction according to their intensity and need.

Goal: Increasing recognition of the emotions in kids.

Instructions for Teacher:

Make four groups or sections of main emotions on the board, i.e., happy, sad, angry, and scared.

- Ask the class to name the most common feelings and write them on the board.
- Now, ask them to think about the questions and answer them.
  - How many of these feelings do you experience in a day?
  - Can you name other emotions that fit into these categories?
- Write down their correct answers on the board in the relevant categories.
- Now, either ask them to draw or hand out the given worksheet provided ahead.

- Tell them to pick one of the emotions from each group and draw them on the blank faces.
- Once everyone has completed the task, ask them to share what they drew and why.

Date: _________________ Day: _________________

Name: _______________ Class: _______________

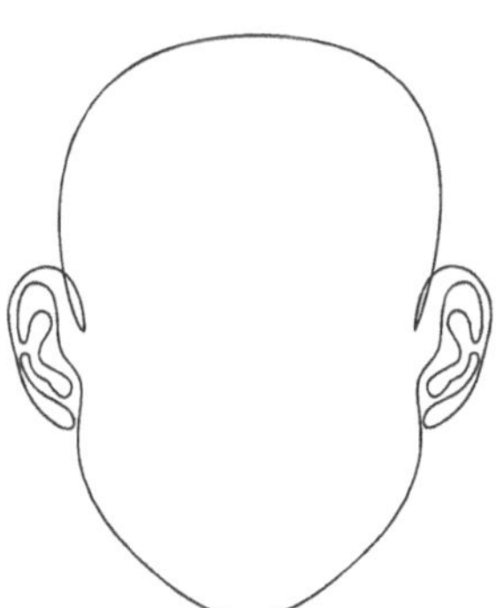

Emotion: _______________

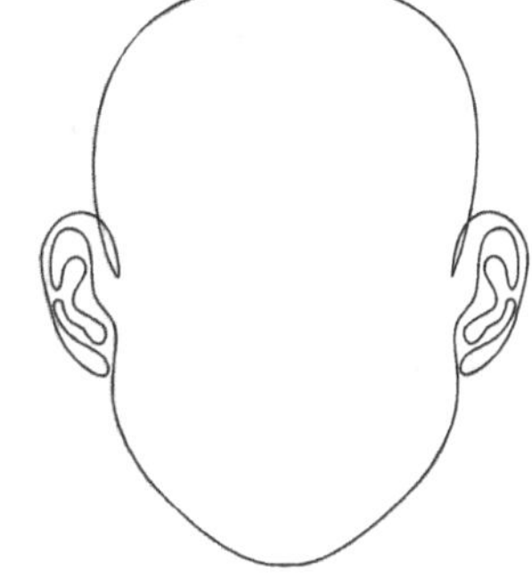

Emotion: _______________

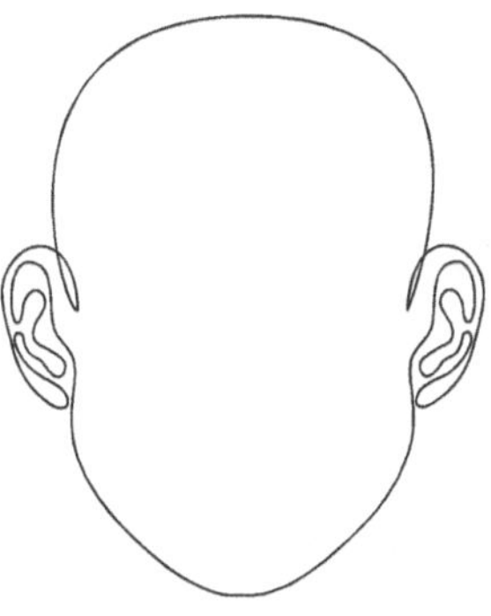

Emotion: _______________

Emotion: _______________

1.2 EXPRESSING THE SITUATIONAL EMOTIONS

Emotions and situations go hand in hand. Any situation can elicit a number of emotions that bombard you instantly. Help kids attach meaning and need to emotions with this exercise.

Goal: Teaching emotional communication that makes each situation bearable.

Instructions for Teacher:

- Stage a brief discussion on how emotions are different in their expressive forms and how kids can express them appropriately.
- Give some situational examples of how emotions vary from each other at different times.
- Share the worksheet with the class and ask them to write down their responses in each situation.
- Once they all complete the task, ask them to share their answers with the class in a healthy discussion.

Date: _______________ Day: _______________

Name: _______________ Class: _______________

If your mom was furious because you didn't finish your homework.

If you failed an exam you studied for.

If you failed an exam without studying.

If you scored 100% on a test.

If your best friend couldn't make it to your birthday party.

If you misplaced your homework.

If someone made fun of you.

If you weren't sure of the answer when your teacher asked you to respond to a question.

1.3 FEELING CONFLICTED...

It is possible to be conflicted about what you feel. You can be happy and sad at the same time. Many situations are too complicated and can make us feel quite confused about our own emotions. Teach the kids to pick out their emotions at any time with the "Feeling Conflicted" exercise.

Goal: Teaching emotional awareness that you can feel more than one emotion at a time.

Instructions for Teacher:

- Tell kids that a person can experience a range of emotions simultaneously. You could be overjoyed to see your friends at school after a long break. But at the same time, be sad that vacations are over. Such things happen all around the world.

- It is important to be conscious of every emotion. Tell them if any of the emotions are bothering them; they can discuss it with anyone they feel comfortable with.

- Share the worksheet with the kids and ask them to identify which emotions the kids feel in there.

- After the kids finish it, gather some volunteers to share times when they felt conflicted about something and ask them to share why.

Date: _______________   Day: _______________

Name: _______________   Class: _______________

I feel: _______
I also feel: _______
My new iPhone was accidentally broken by a friend, but she has promised to get it repaired.
I feel: _______
I also feel: _______
I got a nice birthday gift, but it's not what I wanted.

1.4
TRIGGERS THAT IGNITE THE EMOTIONS

We all have limits. When someone keeps testing your patience, you are bound to explode with feelings that keep piling up, one after another. Tell your students to recognize their thresholds with this activity.

Goal: Finding triggers that are sore spots for children.

Instructions for Teacher:

- Discuss with the class how the emotional capacity makes it difficult to control inner feelings after a certain point.
- Ask all children to consider when they have thought "enough is enough" after experiencing an emotion too much and bursting out on others.
- Distribute the worksheets given ahead to be filled out by students.
- Have a brief discussion after reviewing their answers and clear the concepts if there is any confusion.

Date: _________________   Day: _________________

Name: _________________   Class: _________________

I become irritated when...
How does my body feel?
What I need to do is...

I am confident when...
How does my body feel?
What I need to do is...

It makes me feel ashamed when...
How does my body feel?
What I need to do is...

I get excited when...
How does my body feel?
What I need to do is...

My anger levels rise when...
How does my body feel?
What I need to do is...

I feel happy when...
How does my body feel?
What I need to do is...

It worries me when...
How does my body feel?
What I need to do is...

I am sad when...
How does my body feel?
What I need to do is...

1.5 CONTROLLING THE ANGER WITHIN

Emotions can have a significant impact when they reach the point of no return. You cannot always stay put in difficult situations. It is best to handle the negativity with some positive coping skills.

Goal: Building emotional resilience and finding appropriate coping skills in extreme anger situations.

Instructions for Teacher:

- When you have discussed emotional responses on the whole with the class, tell them to focus more on their anger responses.
- Of all emotions, anger can be the most negative one in terms of getting out of control. Give out the following worksheet that tests their anger management skills.
- Once they have completed the worksheet, go over their answers and discuss how they can manage their anger triggers in a better way.

Recall a recent incident where you lost control of your anger. What happened? What was your reaction? Tell the story here:

____

____

____

____

____

____

____

____

____

Now, pick a sign that could have helped you control your anger in the given situation and fill in the blank.

IT'S NOT A BIG DEAL BECAUSE...

I CAN STAY CALM BY...

I CAN VENT ABOUT MY ANGER WITH...

TAKING A LONG BREATH WILL HELP ME FEEL...

I'M WALKING AWAY, WHICH MAKES ME FEEL...

I CAN DO SOMETHING ELSE RIGHT NOW, SUCH AS...

1.6 EMPATHIZING WITH OTHERS

Show your students how they can learn the art of empathizing with this exercise. Make a case for modifying the actions and behaviors till they are accustomed to showing sympathy and empathy to others around them.

Goal: Teaching children how to truly understand other's emotions and feelings by putting yourself in their shoes.

Instructions for Teacher:

- Explain the concept of empathy and have a discussion that helps kids understand what empathy is.
- Provide them with the worksheet to fill according to their understanding.
- Once everyone has filled out their worksheet, discuss their answers to help clarify the concepts if there is some room left.

What do you suppose Ashley felt when Melanie did not invite her to the party?

____

____

Can you feel empathy towards Ashley's situation?

____

____

Have you ever experienced anything similar?

____

____

In your opinion, how did Jake feel when he was not selected for the team?

____

____

Can you feel empathy towards Jake's situation?

____

____

Have you ever experienced anything similar?

____

____

What do you think Laura's mom felt when Laura didn't pay attention to her?

____

____

Can you feel empathy towards Laura's situation?

____

____

Have you ever experienced anything similar?

____

____

How do you suppose Mark felt when Scott teased him?

____

____

Can you feel empathy towards Mark's situation?

____

____

Have you ever experienced anything similar?

____

____

Emotions are hard for some people. If you see your students in need of help with expressing their emotions, guide them to show those big emotions with a doodling session in class.

Goal: Finding alternative ways to express emotions.

Instructions for Teacher:

- Provide the students with blank sheets of paper or a chart and ask them to fill them up with doodles of their choice.

- It could be doodles of anything that helps them let go of an emotion that keeps bugging them.

- Once everyone is done, ask everyone to go to the front of the class and present their doodles.

- Ask the following questions:
  - What have you drawn?
  - Which emotion drove you to draw this doodle?

As you can guess from the name, this activity will help kids identify and recognize emotions by looking at nonverbal and external cues.

Goal: Recognizing emotional responses from body language and images.

Instructions for Teacher:

- It is a fairly easy exercise. Distribute the worksheets, one at a time, to kids in the class and ask them to write down a detailed description of the story unfolding in the picture.
- Ask them to pay close attention to facial expressions.
- Once they have written descriptions, check the worksheet to note their observational skills.
- Discuss the image in class to give students a clear understanding of if they were wrong in their assessment.
- Bonus points for anyone coming up with creative story ideas for the background of the pictures on how they reached those particular scenes and what can happen next.

1.9
PRACTICING GIVE-AND-TAKE

Give-and-take phenomenon has been around for a long time. It is best to reach compromises that benefit both and help solve the issue without disturbing anyone. Teach give and take to students through this activity.

Goal: Finding solutions to the everyday problems that can arise anytime.

Instructions for Teacher:

- Have a discussion with the class on the topic of compromise. Ask them to share what is compromising in their eyes and if they have practiced it themselves.
- Share the worksheets with them to fill out.
- Have a session afterward where each student gets to show their responses to the class and explain why they believe it is the best solution for the case.

Date: _______________   Day: _______________

Name: _______________   Class: _______________

Is it possible for these children to reach an agreement? Write your response in the spaces between the kids in each example and come up with a solution.

1.10 UNWINDING WITH HOBBIES

Hobbies can help find a regulation in the emotional chaos that helps the kids find emotional support in times of severe emotional distress. Help your students find their favorite hobbies to find their support system.

Goal: An alternative option that encompasses finding the right passion that helps with emotional regulation.

Instructions for Teacher:

- Ask your students to distribute the worksheet given ahead in class and name the hobbies they would love to try.
- Ask them to explain their reasons, too.
- Count the most popular activities in your class and pick any one or two to perform in class if you have all the supplies or if there is no need for them.
- Have a great time with kids to allow them to bond over their love of the same hobbies.

- You could also give them homework on taking up some purposeful hobby at home and report their progress to you each day.

<table>
<tr><td>Date: _______________</td><td>Day: _______________</td></tr>
<tr><td>Name: _______________</td><td>Class: _______________</td></tr>
</table>

Name ten hobbies that you would like to try but haven't had a chance to do so before.

____

____

____

____

____

____

____

____

Give your reasons.

1.11
BONUS:
MINDFULNESS COLORING TO CALM THE MIND

Coloring is a simple yet effective approach to learning and practicing mindfulness. If you see your students struggling with emotional regulation, allow them to spend some time with this relaxing activity.

Goal: Finding alternative artistic ways to let go of intense emotions.

Instructions for Teacher:

- Provide the worksheets to students and ask them to use colored pencils to fill the shape with beautiful colors.
- Once they complete the activity, tell them to post their drawings on the class softboard or to take them to their homes and put them there.
- You can also ask them to write personalized messages that can inspire them when feeling down. It will motivate them or others when in need of some cheering.

Date: _______________   Day: _______________

Name: _______________   Class: _______________

Date: _______________   Day: _______________

Name: _______________   Class: _______________

COMPONENT 2

SOCIAL SKILLS

It is extremely important to make kids more adaptable in their social life because any school-going child is in the golden age of learning the social norms that are very limited in home life. If they are pushed in the right direction, they have the skills to form acquaintanceships and friendships that can get them through the tough times.

The activities and games provided in this section will help you get your students out of their comfort zones gradually without pressuring them to form meaningless links. Instead, they will show these students how they can have a good time with others in class or school if they allow themselves to enjoy such games.

2.1 INTENSE STARING CHALLENGE

It is a perfect game for kids who are hesitant or shy in class. They can learn to keep eye contact with others during conversation and other matters through this challenge. The key is to not push kids too much but try to bring them out of their shells slowly and steadily.

Goal: Building eye contact skills in kids through this fun game.

Instructions for Teacher:

- Pair the kids in teams of two.
- Explain the rules of the game that they must not touch the other person or try to distract them in any way. Whoever blinks first loses the game.
- Then, set two chairs facing each other at the front of the class and ask each pair to come and sit at the chairs.
- Start the timer and tell all other students to keep an eye on the challengers.

- Play the game randomly or make it into round matches that go up to the semi-finals and final that ultimately a child wins (you can set a prize for the winner, too).

This activity involves the mimicking of the expression that most kids love anyway. It is one of those silly and fun-loving games that keep kids entertained. Similar to the previous activity, you can pair kids here or play with the whole class simultaneously.

Goal: Learning the importance of using the right facial expressions in different situations.

Instructions for Teacher:

- Either make pairs or appoint someone to come and stand in front of the class.
- Ask them to make any expressions they like with their face while others have to copy their every move.
- Progressively, you or the appointed person can make gestures difficult to follow to make the game more interesting.

2.3 FINDING COMMON LIKES

Commonalities are hard to find when you are not willing to open up to others. Use this activity to help kids break the ice and start making friends with their peers.

Goal: Identifying common likes and dislikes that encourage communication.

Instructions for Teacher:

- Give out the worksheets to the students and ask them to identify the things in each section that they love.
- Based on their answers, pair them with someone who has chosen similar answers in one or more categories to try and find three or more similarities.
- Encourage them to have conversations and share their views of different things to land on some ground.

Date: _______________   Day: _______________

Name: _______________   Class: _______________

I enjoy playing...

Football

Hockey

Basketball

Tennis

Baseball

Other: _______________

My favorite pastime is...

Playing Video Games

Writing

Enjoying Some Music

Reading

Spending Time with Friends

Other: _______________

I enjoy eating...

Chinese Cuisine

Indian Cuisine

Japanese Cuisine

Italian Cuisine

Southern American Cuisine

Other: _______________

My favorite subject is...

Mathematics

English

Science

History

Arts

Other: _______________

When I grow up, I want to be...	I live with...
Teacher	Parent
Firefighter	My Sister
Doctor	My Brother
Businessperson	Adoptive Parent
A Professional Athlete	Grandparent(s)
Other: _______________	Other: _______________

2.4 INTERACTIVE ROLE-PLAYING GAME

Think of it as the imitation of your teachings. If you can get children to take up other characters to behave a bit differently, it is possible that they will interact in that role, performing more social norms than they normally do.

Goal: Building social skills through characterizing and play.

Instructions for Teacher:

- In this game, you can start small, maybe by asking them to imitate a monkey or a lion in this first session. It will help them ease into the role-playing.

- Gradually make your students more comfortable with a popular story or cartoons that like to re-enact the scenes from it.

- Swap the roles regularly to give them a challenge each time. It will allow them to not think about their performance rather than just doing it for the sake of fun and games in class.

- Who knows, it might make them comfortable enough to put on a play in front of the whole school by next year.

2.5 ON-THE-SPOT STORYTELLING

Storytelling can make kids work on their critical thinking skills along with socializing in the same-age group setting. It will help them learn to interact with others to have a good time together. It will enhance their collaboration skills.

Goal: Learning to take social cues and giving appropriate responses.

Instructions for Teacher:

- In this game, you can start small, maybe by asking them to imitate a monkey or a lion in this first session. It will help them ease into the role-playing.
- Gradually make your students more comfortable with a popular story or cartoons that like to re-enact the scenes from it.
- Swap the roles regularly to give them a challenge each time. It will allow them to not think about their performance rather than just doing it for the sake of fun and games in class.

2.6 GROUP GARDENING ACTIVITY

A gardening activity can help children learn how to take care of other living things and to do so with competence. It will allow them to care for and nurture other than themselves for once.

Goal: Learning about working together in outdoor settings.

Instructions for Teacher:

- Organize a workshop for the kids that tell them about different plants and their growth time.
- Show or tell them the process of planting.
- Pick a spot that is perfect for planting different plants, and tell the students to pick any of the plants you provide to plant themselves.
- You may form groups to build teamwork skills.
- You can also ask them to note the date and keep track of the plant's growth. They may give a small presentation on how long it took to grow leaves, flowers, etc.
- They can also make and decorate a fence around it to stake their claim.

2.7 LETTER-SWAPPING GAME

Letter swapping can help you improve the writing skills of your class, along with teaching them the art of communicating with others in a written manner. It will help you educate them by building lasting bonds in their age group.

Goal: Cultivating written communication skills in kids.

Instructions for Teacher:

- Put the names of everyone in the class on chits. Fold and put them in a bowl and mix them up.
- Now, tell everyone in class to pick a chit. They should only see and not tell the names they have got.
- Tell them to start writing letters to the person you got in chit. It should be a pleasant letter that does not insult or be rude to the other person.
- Ask them to submit letters to you, and you can do a daily giveaway at the start or end of the day.

- The letters should be anonymous so that no one feels ashamed or shy of holding a realistic conversation with the other.
- You may keep this activity going for a week or a month to improve your writing skills.

2.8 CHINESE WHISPER – DANCING STYLE

You surely have heard about Chinese whisper by now. It is a fun game that many people enjoy. This is the same thing here but with an interesting twist. You need to get your students moving and having fun while forming great memories together.

Goal: Building friendship and closeness in students.

Instructions for Teacher:

- Gather around the class in a straight line and tell the last person to do a few dance steps while the person standing before has to turn around and see the dance to copy it for the next person.
- Everyone should follow the steps they have seen and get to the end. It is a hysterical variation of Chinese whisper that kids will enjoy a lot.

2.9 SCATTERED INSTRUCTIONS GAME

"Scattered Instructions Game" is essential in making groups of students work together while bartering the things they need for what others need. It is a mock trial of situations they will face in real life. It is up to them to convince each other to provide help.

Goal: Learning the trade of coordination and planning to reach individualized goals.

Instructions for Teacher:

- Write down or print the instructions for doing a project, such as origami, art-making of any kind, etc., to be performed in groups. You can also color code the instructions to make it easier to find the scattered instructions.
- You may make groups of two or more students and assign different projects to different teams.

- Ask the groups to coordinate with each other to complete their set of instructions.
- They may start making their projects once the instructions are complete.

2.10
QUIZ OF QUERIES

Making queries and asking questions is part of the norm. If you are looking to educate your students on becoming an effective conversationalist, this exercise is best. It will help them become socially adept.

Goal: Teaching the questioning aspect of conversation by following the logical thought progression.

Instructions for Teacher:

- Talk about making conversations in class. Talk with some examples of how they should carry on conversations. It could be a realistic observation of a situation, or you could ask them to start talking to you on any matter.

- Once the concept is clear, give them worksheets to fill out.

- Ask the students to read the instructions carefully and complete the task.

Here's a possible conversation starter with your friend or any other person. Complete reading the dialogues and then continue the conversation by coming up with three more questions and their responses.

You: Have you seen my cat?   Your Friend: No.Where did
                                                  you see him last?

You: He was sitting on the bed   Your Friend: When was that?
     when I saw him.

You: An hour ago.   Your Friend: ________________

You: ________________   Your Friend: ________________

You: ________________   Your Friend: ________________

You: ________________   Your Friend: ________________

Now, make a conversation with five prompts from each side and draw a relevant picture to describe the situation.

2.11 BONUS: FOCUSED LISTENING

Listening is an integral part of effective communication and social skills. Learning this skill will help your students to have the best prospects of making and keeping friends for a long time.

Goal: Teaching basics of active listening for future usage.

Instructions for Teacher:

- Discuss the importance of active listening in class. Give a few examples to clarify the concept.
- Once clarified, provide the worksheet to the class. Ask them to fill it out after reading the conversations properly.
- If they are confused or have questions, answer them to assist their focused listening skills.

It appears that not all of the kids are paying attention to their friends. Circle the pairs that are equally invested in the conversation.

COMPONENT ③

SELF MANAGEMENT

Self-management stems from building a realistic viewpoint of what you are and which skills you need to build to live a successful life ahead. Making students able to manage themselves according to the situation they face can be the most valuable skill they could ever acquire.

Thoughts, behaviors, and emotions can all be conformed to by using the worksheets and activities provided ahead in the given section. It allows you to give some food for thought to the students who struggle with controlling one or more aspects of their lives.

3.1 ADAPTING TO CHANGE

Change happens every day. We must be equipped to handle the ever-changing experiences of life, no matter what happens. That's why it is necessary to help students become the best version of themselves by being prepared for the unexpected.

Goal: Conforming to change and accepting it as part of life.

Instructions for Teacher:

- Discuss and ask the students about their perspective on change in general.
- Give them open space and authority so they can share their ideas in a controlled environment.
- Provide them with worksheets to give answers.

Date: _________________   Day: _________________

Name: _________________   Class: _________________

In each scenario, how would you feel? How can you respond to the change in a constructive way?

I would feel____________.
I could________________
____
____

I would feel____________.
I could________________
____
____

Our behavior helps us be distinct from all other people around us. Everyone leaves an impact in each interaction they have with other people. If you are nice to others, they will remember that, and in the same way, if you are rude to them, they will judge you for that, too. Teach the students to always be nice and courteous to others to leave a good impression on them.

Goal: Teaching the impact and effects of our behavior on others.

Instructions for Teacher:

- It can be difficult for some kids to identify how their behavior affects others in their daily lives. Show them how their words and actions can make or break someone's day by discussing a few examples in class.

- Once they are familiar with both the positive and negative impact they can have on others, ask them to fill out the worksheets on their own. It will help strengthen their concepts.

For each situation, consider whether the actions of the first person would be good or bad for the second person. Next, choose the appropriate column and enter a checkmark there. Fill the blanks below with your own examples.

	Positive Effects	Negative Effects
Lucy eats George's lunch without his permission.	_______________	_______________
Andrew borrows some glitter markers from Helen.	_______________	_______________
Gary brings back a book that Michael misplaced.	_______________	_______________
Kevin cheats the exam by looking over John's paper.	_______________	_______________
Fred gets distracted by Julia bouncing her leg in class.	_______________	_______________
Peter laughed when Tom crashed his bike.	_______________	_______________
When Evelyn has homework, Tanya helps her out.	_______________	_______________
On the baseball field, Nora makes fun of Daisy.	_______________	_______________

3.3
HEART OF KINDNESS

This activity is a promising attempt to foster kindness and goodwill in children for each other. It will help them find goodness in each other and give their appreciation where it is due.

Goal: Encouraging kindness in students and providing reasons to spread kindness in class.

Instructions for Teacher:

- Print as many given worksheets as you can to give out one to each student.
- Write down the names of each student or ask them to write themselves and shuffle the hearts.
- Ask all students to pick one heart each and write a kind gesture they can do for that person. It could be a compliment, a nice action, or anything else that can make them feel appreciated.

Date: _______________ Day: _______________

Name: _______________ Class: _______________

3.4 FORMING A POSITIVE MINDSET

A positive attitude and mindset come from building the reasons for improvement rather than demoralizing by focusing on the negatives. It comes from identifying the difficulties that kids face in their lives and giving importance to the aspects that can be improved with hard work.

Goal: Learning to keep a positive attitude in areas that need improvement on their part.

Instructions for Teacher:

- Discuss what it means to have a positive outlook on life. Having a positive mindset can have a good impact on the quality of their mental and physical health. Discuss that as well.
- Once done, ask them to distribute and fill out the worksheet given ahead.
- Ask them to share their answers with the rest of the class one by one and tell others what they have written and why.

Date: _______________   Day: _______________

Name: _______________   Class: _______________

Put three things you'd like to improve or alter about yourself in the left column. Consider these items with a more optimistic outlook and record your thoughts or drawings in the right column.

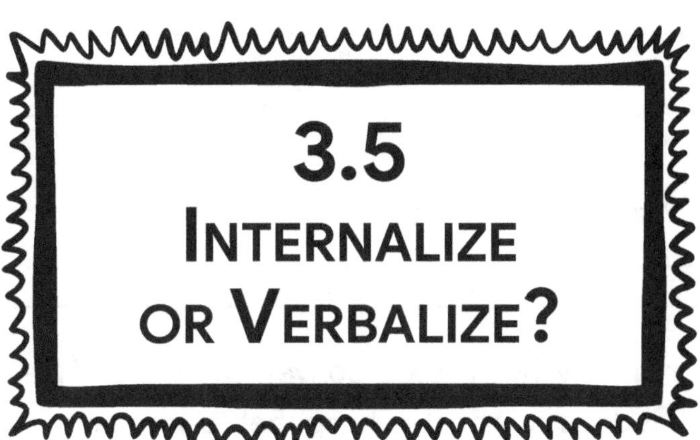

Saying and thinking are two completely different processes, and learning the clear distinction between them is a necessary skill that each person needs to learn. If a person needs to know what to say and when to say it, tell them to take a beat and think if they should voice their thoughts or not.

Goal: Learning the difference between appropriate and inappropriate responses in interactions with other people.

Instructions for Teacher:

- Ask the students about what they do when a person behaves in any manner that could be commented upon.
- Take the discussion further from their responses and talk about why it is important to learn the right responses for any situation.
- Give out the worksheets to students and ask them to complete them to the best of their understanding.

Our words may not always convey the exact meaning we intend. If it does, it is best to keep that to yourself.

Consider the following statements and choose which ones you would want to internalize (think) or express aloud (say). Feel free to also provide a few phrases of your own!

- You look hilarious in this dress today.
- I didn't mean that.
- I won't sit with you.
- You're being impolite.
- You can't compete with me at this.
- Sorry, but I disagree with you.
- That was excellent work.
- Please explain yourself; I'm confused.
- I am not having a good day today.
- Do you have any idea what you're doing?
- I'm struggling to understand this.

INTERNALIZE IT	VERBALIZE IT

3.6 MARKING MY LIMITS

We all have a few personal boundaries and limits that play a key role in making us comfortable in talking and interacting with others. Some are comfortable in shaking hands with strangers; others might be uncomfortable hugging even the closest of their loved ones.

Find out your students' limits by doing this activity.

Goal: Discovering the comfort zones of everyone in class to make sure they are not breached.

Instructions for Teacher:

- Have a small session with the class on what boundaries are and how they can be enforced within their social circle.
- Ask them to monitor and report the actions that make them uncomfortable in any situation.
- Appoint one student to give out the worksheets and ask them to fill these according to their opinions and feelings.

Date: ______________   Day: ______________

Name: ______________   Class: ______________

Checkmark the boxes where you are comfortable performing that action. If you do not feel comfortable with any of the given actions, leave them blank.

	Actions are Acceptable for...		
	Family	Friends	Strangers
Shaking Hands			
High-fives			
Holding Hands with Someone			
Hugging			
Sitting Very Close to Another Person			
Someone Touching My Stuff			

3.7 ANALYZING THE ACTIONS

It is inevitable for students to get in some fight eventually where they deviate from being at model behavior. If any student needs to self-reflect on their actions, ask them to go through this worksheet and see what is bothering them and why.

Goal: Giving students a chance for self-reflection and self-awareness.

Instructions for Teacher:

- When a fight erupts in your class that is either verbal or physical, get out this worksheet to get their opinions on their own behavior.
- It will help them go over the incident till they can find the cause that triggered them.
- It will also allow them to make and follow potential strategies that can help them next time they are triggered.

Date: _________________   Day: _________________

Name: _________________   Class: _________________

Make a picture of what took place. Select the option that describes why this activity is not permitted at school.

	This behavior is unacceptable because:	
	It is unsafe.	
	This is not kind.	
	It caused pain/harm to someone.	
	It caused property damage.	
	It interfered with learning.	
	It goes against the regulations of our school.	

When this occurred, how did you feel?

____

____

Make a note of some potential responses in case this occurs again.

____

____

____

____

3.8 CONTROLLING THE REACTIONS

It is necessary for kids to understand when their reactions are under their control and when not. If you are looking for some ways to teach your students about which reactions and behaviors are appropriate in any given situation, use this activity to let the situation work out in their favor.

Goal: Finding clear distinction between responses and reactions that state the control level in kids.

Instructions for Teacher:

- Talk to your students and ask them to share some examples of situations where they had to control themselves from bursting out.
- Ask them about what they did and the reasons behind their actions.
- Discuss how the situations warranted their actions or reactions and how to identify which reactions are more appropriate for them.
- Distribute the worksheet to be filled out and see if their concepts are clear or not.

Date: _______________   Day: _______________

Name: _______________   Class: _______________

The following are some reactions you could have while you are feeling in or out of control. If you are having trouble identifying your reaction, feel free to add your own when you use the chart to organize them.

Responses

Walking Quickly or Pacing	Rapid Heartbeat	Sitting Quietly
Getting Away from the Situation	Breathing Slowly	Screaming and Shouting.
Feeling Lightheaded	Mental Count Down	Destroying Things
Paying Attention	Punching and Hitting	Acting Politely
Following the Regulations	Engaging in Conversations with Friends	

Under Control	Not Under Control	Both

3.9 SELF-CARE SAFETY PROTOCOL

It is important to know which things, activities, and people are most trustworthy by a child to ensure their safety and security.

If any of your students are finding it difficult to build some sort of attachment to things and people, you may ask them to identify what constitutes their safe zone. It can help you in bringing them out of their shell.

This activity is a low-pressure exercise that allows kids to feel safe and secure.

Goal: Naming the things, people, and activities that can allow children to feel safe in an environment.

Instructions for Teacher:

- Ask the students what their safe space is and what features it has that makes it so.

- Listen to their opinions and have a healthy discussion on why it is important to feel a need for secure place/people in life.
- Make a plan on why it is necessary to indicate the things that make you feel secure, and then give out the worksheets to talk about their necessity in everyone's healthy growth and development.

Date: _________________ Day: _________________

Name: _________________ Class: _________________

Things that make me feel secure include...

1. _________________

2. _________________

3. _________________

4. _________________

When I am in danger, my body alerts me by...

1. _________________

2. _________________

3. _________________

Adults that I can trust completely are...

1. _________________

2. _________________

3. _________________

4. _________________

5. _________________

6. _________________

7. _________________

8. _________________

9. _________________

The following activities contribute to making me feel safe...

1. _______________________________
2. _______________________________
3. _______________________________
4. _______________________________
5. _______________________________
6. _______________________________
7. _______________________________
8. _______________________________
9. _______________________________
10. _______________________________
11. _______________________________
12. _______________________________
13. _______________________________
14. _______________________________
15. _______________________________
16. _______________________________
17. _______________________________
18. _______________________________

3.10 HONORING THE ACHIEVEMENTS

Most of the students work very hard to stay on top of their grades, learning easy and relevant skills, manners, and everything in between to make sure they are nice and polite to everyone they meet.

These small things matter a lot in growing age and should be acknowledged by others and by themselves equally. Allow the students to honor themselves by going through the "Honoring the Achievements" worksheet.

Goal: Giving credit where it is due, with positive thinking and self-assessment in play.

Instructions for Teacher:

- Have a class session with the students where they discuss how they practice some good behaviors in school and at home.
- Make sure to tell the students to interact with each other to make it a successful session.

- Distribute the worksheets to ask the students about what they are proud of in themselves.

Date: _________________   Day: _________________

Name: _________________   Class: _________________

I, (name) _________________,

accomplished something very remarkable.

I (describe your actions)

____

____.

I felt (describe your emotional reaction)

____

____

at that moment.

Congrats to me!

3.11 BONUS: STAYING COOL AND CALM

Each situation asks for a different response. Some of those responses are healthy, while others are unhealthy. Learn more about your students coping skills by judging their strategies for dealing with adverse situations.

Goal: Learning alternative practices in staying calm in trying situations.

Instructions for Teacher:

- Give out the worksheets for students to fill out. Ask them to return those when they are done.
- Get to know the emotional and physical toll your students experience in some negative situations by studying their responses on the worksheet.
- Discuss which strategies they have used and if they have ever worked for them in class.

<table>
<tr><td>Date: _______________</td><td>Day: _______________</td></tr>
<tr><td>Name: _______________</td><td>Class: _______________</td></tr>
</table>

The Situation	Describe Your Mood with an Emoji	A Strategy That Could Help You Calm Down
When I requested to play outside, I was told "no" by my mother.		_______________ _______________
I made a mistake in front of the entire class.		_______________ _______________
My favorite toy is broken and cannot be repaired.		_______________ _______________
I need to go to the doctor to get a shot.		_______________ _______________
At school, someone picked on me and called me a nasty name.		_______________ _______________

COMPONENT ④

CRITICAL THINKING

When it comes to thinking critically, almost all students have a distinct type of personality that allows them to think about different objects, situations, and people from various aspects. Let's take you for an example. When you are stuck in traffic, you might be thinking about getting home and lying down while someone else is thinking about taking the next U-turn and getting out of the traffic jam through another way.

It is all about having varying perspectives while encountering a similar situation. That's what makes humans unique to each other. They give different and most creative responses to situations that most wouldn't even think about.

This section will help you polish these critical thinking skills in your students through the given content.

4.1 INTERNALIZE OR VERBALIZE?

(Best to be paired with activity 4.2)

Giving free rein to thoughts and ideas is the main part of allowing the mind to take a few tries to reach an optimal solution that solves the issues. If your students need help with keeping up with their thoughts, show them the easy way of brainstorming ideas and choosing the best from the rest.

Goal: Finding multiple solutions for one problem and solving it with the best possible solution at hand.

Instructions for Teacher:

- Ask the students the following questions:
    - What do they do when there is an issue to solve?
    - How does their thought process work? Ask for examples of any recent problems they solved.
    - Are they familiar with the concept of brainstorming? If not, explain it in detail.

- Distribute the worksheets to have them brainstorm any issue that they are facing either at home or school.

Date: _________________   Day: _________________

Name: _________________   Class: _________________

The Issue: _________________________________

4.2 SEEKING OTHER OPTIONS

Although we chose one option in the brainstorming session that seemed most suitable according to the situation, there can still be many options that are appropriate for one problem.

For example, if you are looking for a temporary housing situation for a stray cat, you can give it a cardboard box to snuggle into, or a blanket, or both. But you could also let it stay in your house by giving it an old cat bed you were going to throw out. Each situation can have more than one solution that works best.

Goal: Learning dynamic problem-solving skills with diverse solution-making.

Instructions for Teacher:

- Discuss the instances of coming up with more than one viable solution that works in your favor at the time. Ask the students to come up with their own examples of finding more solutions to just one problem.

- Once the session is concluded, ask them to complete the worksheet provided ahead.

Do you have three solutions for each problem? Solve the given issues and then consider an issue that has to be resolved in your life and give three possible solutions for it.

SOLUTION I	SOLUTION II
_______________	_______________

Katie, Jane, and Max are all interested in sitting at the same desk.

SOLUTION III

____

SOLUTION I	SOLUTION II
_______________	_______________

Jimmy forgets to turn in his school homework on its due date.

SOLUTION III

____

SOLUTION I	SOLUTION II
_______________	_______________

I need to solve the following problem:

SOLUTION III

____

4.3 STARTING THE CHAIN ACTIVITY

You may play this "Starting the Chain" activity in several ways, but the most popular one is to pick a topic and then use the letters of the alphabet to name objects that are included in that category.

Goal: Quick and interactive thinking that teaches instant response time.

Instructions for Teacher:

- Gather the students and tell them to pick a few main topics they can use for this activity. If your theme is animals, you may start by naming animals like:
  - A: Ape
  - B: Bear
  - C: Crow
- Tell students to focus on this single task at playing time and follow instructions to the letter.

- Start the game after giving places to each person in the class and ask them to wait for their turn.
- Keep going until no one can think of any other objects from the chosen activity.

The aliens are visiting the human world, and they need your students to make a tour manual that tells them everything they need to know about this planet.

Taking part in this activity will help the students to examine their personal and collective identities in greater detail. It's all about taking a step back and seeing our behavior and values through a fresh pair of eyes.

Goal: Fostering critical thinking and creativity through group projects.

Instructions for Teacher:

- Using the scenarios, ask them to come up with convincing answers and then make a collective guide of at least ten pages that tells the alien about the workings of the planet Earth.
- First, give the worksheet to students and ask them to provide interesting answers.

- Then, tell the students to pick some topics they think are the most important for an alien to learn about this planet.
- Ask them to take one topic each and make their parts to form a manual booklet.
- They may make it in question and answers format as given here or give details on their own.

Date: _______________   Day: _______________

Name: _______________   Class: _______________

Answering the questions in each exercise is a great opportunity to dig deeper into beliefs and aspects of daily life we often take for granted. Two examples are given. Answer the given questions to the best of your abilities.

Situation 1

Aliens are visiting Earth to study human life, and you are their tour guide. A spaceship carrying all of you passes above a football stadium. It looks like one of the aliens is lost and needs your help. Give his questions a go:

What are games, and why do all humans play them?

____

____

____

Why do humans need "teams" to play?

____

____

____

Why do these games attract greater interest than sickness and poverty on this planet?

____

____

____

Why do people become so worked up and even aggressive when watching sports?

____

____

____

What if humans could never play such games again?

____

____

____

____

____

Situation 2

You are giving a local library tour and having a conversation with some aliens. While you are all mingling, one of the aliens grabs a book on the history of worldwide conflict and division. The alien faces you and asks:

Why do people go to battle with one another, and what exactly is war?

____

____

____

War seems to be the only option that humans choose when faced with an issue. How come?

____

____

____

How are winners and losers chosen? How can you be sure that this is true?

____

____

____

____

____

What happens to those who choose not to or are unable to take part in a war?

____

____

____

How do you think these conflicts will be remembered by the generations to come?

____

____

____

4.5 CHALLENGING MEMORY GAME

Recalling skills are essential to focus upon when the kids are in the age range of reaching their maximum potential of memorizing and remembering information. It is another activity that targets critical thinking in kids and allows them to work on strengthening their minds with constant practice.

Goal: Testing the remembering and recalling skills of all students.

Instructions for Teacher:

- Tell the students to look at the worksheets provided to them and try to memorize the given words and objects before writing them down.

- It will challenge their memory and recalling skills while having a healthy little competition between class members.

Date: _________________   Day: _________________

Name: _________________   Class: _________________

Look at the given words and objects for one whole minute and try to memorize each thing. After the minute has passed, write down the names of all the things you memorized.

Lion

Tail

Baby

Wings

Bean

Ground

4.6 WITTY LABELS AND DESCRIPTIONS

The "Witty Labels and Descriptions" activity is a great way of bringing an engaging and lively exercise that makes kids use their creative and critical thinking skills. It will encourage them to have a fun time with others by making and reading some fun ideas that all of them come up for this activity.

Goal: Fostering creative thinking in kids.

Instructions for Teacher:

- Give out the worksheets to students and ask them to think and write relevant and funny descriptions of each picture.

- Explain them that it is not necessary to explain the picture but to write something that gives a funny and witty take on it. Consider it a form of commentary but with the minimum possible words.

- Tell them to read aloud their labels to have a great time together with all.

Date: _______________   Day: _______________

Name: _______________   Class: _______________

4.7 WORD REARRANGEMENT GAME

It is quite an easy activity that requires a minimum amount of help. Strengthen your students' basic critical reasoning by making them use their minds to find alternative ones from the given ones.

Easy enough, right?

Goal: Using word rearrangement to develop reasoning skills.

Instructions for Teacher:

- Give out the worksheets to kids to solve on their own.
- See how they answer the worksheet based on their thinking.

Date: _________________ Day: _________________

Name: _________________ Class: _________________

Rearrange the given words to make other words from it. Make at least five for each word. They must have three or more words from the given letters to be acceptable.

Reside	Drown	Later	Part
________	________	________	________
________	________	________	________
________	________	________	________
________	________	________	________
________	________	________	________

Camper	Tarts	Harming	Stairs
________	________	________	________
________	________	________	________
________	________	________	________
________	________	________	________
________	________	________	________

Growing up, a few skills can come in handy in times of need or crisis. Navigational skills are among this long list. Teach direction-giving and reading skills through the activity "Do You Know the Way."

Goal: Building thinking and reasoning skills.

Instructions for Teacher:

- Distribute the worksheet to students and ask them to give directions to any place in the school.

- Tell them not to mention any names and tell them how to get there.

- Now, tell everyone to swap their worksheets with another student.

- They have to make a map now from the directions given on the sheet they received.

- Ask them to go on the adventure of finding the place or write down their answers of which place the other student has given direction to.

- Now, ask them to re-swap the papers to recheck who figured out the directions correctly and who did not.

Date: _______________   Day: _______________

Name: _______________   Class: _______________

Player 1: _______________

Player 2: _______________

Write down directions to a place within the school grounds. Swap the worksheet with another player. Make a map from their given directions. Write down the destination name once you know.

For Player 1

Directions to a Place within the School:

____

____

____

For Player 2

The Map:

Destination: _______________

4.9 TESTING THE NUMBERS KNOWLEDGE

Solving basic math functions at your fingertips is the easiest method of learning memorization. This activity will help kids get more proficient in doing math, along with listening and following directions in a fast-paced environment.

Goal: Developing listening and following skills in kids.

Instructions for Teacher:

- Give main instructions to students that they must listen to the instructions provided ahead and write their answers down as they go along.
- They must understand the meaning of instructions by listening to you carefully and comprehending what it means.
- Tell them to take out papers and start writing.
- You may modify the game by making it easier or more difficult according to the caliber of your students.

Instructions for Students:

Give these instructions to students when they are ready to play.

- Write any number. For instance, 52. (52)
- Count ahead five numbers. (57)
- Skip one line, and count back three numbers. (54)
- Count two backward, ten ahead, and skip four lines. (62)
- Count back nine numbers and skip another line. (53)
- Skip two lines, count ahead five numbers, count back two numbers, and skip one line. (56)
- Count back four numbers. (52)
- What is the new number? (52)

4.10
THE LAST BATTLE PREPARATION

Having an imaginative and creative idea to work through a situation can help them become more and more accustomed to decision-making in tough situations. It will allow them to formulate reasonable assumptions and use their mind to make through similar scenarios they may face in adult life.

Goal: Practice of logical and rational thinking skills to plan things beforehand.

Instructions for Teacher:

- Ask the students to fill out the given worksheet.
- Tell them to think long and hard before making decisions and give logical reasons for each decision.
- Once kids are done, look at their worksheets to see how they did it.

Date: _______________   Day: _______________

Name: _______________   Class: _______________

Let's say that you are an astronaut and you want to set up a new colony on planet Mars. But there are bad aliens who will not share it with you. Think about how you will proceed by filling out this worksheet.

Write down your name, rank, and your mission name here.

Name: _________________________________

Rank: _______________   Mission Name: _______________

What skills do you think you and your team members will need to not only survive on Mars but build a functional home there?

Needed Skills   Reasons

_______________   _________________________________

_______________   _________________________________

_______________   _________________________________

_______________   _________________________________

You will need a few trusted members in your squad to lead the mission and make it habitable for humans. Who will you pick, and what jobs would you offer them?

Persons   Job Designation(s)

_______________   _________________________________

_______________   _________________________________

4.11 BONUS: THE FASCINATING NUMBER SQUARES

Numbers and critical thinking go hand in hand because such simple addition is one of the most basic functions that we all encounter every day. It can be a learning experience for students, along with a bundle of joy.

Goal: Fostering calculation abilities in kids.

Instructions for Teacher:

- There are a few rules for playing this game. Tell these to your students before starting the game:
  - Number Squares are always equal in the sum values from rows and columns.
  - No number can be used twice.
- Give out the worksheets and start having fun.

Sum Number: 18

9		
		8
5		3

Sum Number: 15

2		4
6	1	

Sum Number: 45

	21	
3		27
		12

Sum Number: 24

11		7
	8	
	10	

Sum Number: 30

12	2	
4		8

Sum Number: 21

6		10
11		
	9	

COMPONENT 5

DECISION MAKING

Decision-making is a hard skill to master, no matter what your age is. If your kids need to learn how to make valuable decisions at any given moment, SEL is the best practice to acquire this skill.

Having a necessary ideation of what they can do to analyze the situation and the after-effects it will produce are the two main aspects of any decision. If you teach them these bare minimums, they are most likely to become self-aware of all their existing options and potential aftermaths they will face. By introducing the activities given in this section, you can make them more certain of their choices and have the courage to stand by those choices whenever they are questioned.

5.1 RATING YOUR DECISION-MAKING SKILLS

The decision-making process is secondary to knowing where one stands in decision-making skills. If someone is not used to making decisions, it may take them a long time to get there without support.

Teach your students to build their life skills by letting them find their hidden talents and reasoning that seldom come out on their own.

Goal: Self-evaluation of skills and thought processes behind decision-making.

Instructions for Teacher:

- Have a small discussion in class about why decisions are important and how they can shape the future.
- Give away the worksheet to students and ask them to fill it according to their understanding.

Date: _________________   Day: _________________

Name: _______________   Class: _______________

Give yourself a score in decision-making skills *(10 being the highest - 1 being the lowest)*.

____

Give an example that comes to your mind in terms of the best decision-making skills you have used in life. It could be an example of your decision-making skills in your own interest or other's.

____

____

____

____

____

What do you think it means to be responsible in the decision-making process? Explain your thoughts.

____

____

____

Give any example of decisions you took for yourself that made you better at handling emotions, thoughts, or behavior.

____

____

____

____

Is there any reason why you think your decision-making is sound? If yes, how?

____

____

____

____

5.2 MUST-FOLLOW RULES

Get to know the thought processes and workings of your students' minds by giving them a fun activity, "Must-Follow Rules." It will help them narrow down and choose their answers by looking at the most usable rules that can be important for them or someone/something related to them.

Goal: Choosing relevant answers based on thought processes.

Instructions for Teacher:

- Distribute the worksheet to students and ask them to fill it.
- Ask them to give good reasons for choosing the rules they write.
- You may also conduct a session afterward where each kid comes up to present their proposed rules.

<table>
<tr><td>Date: _______________</td><td>Day: _______________</td></tr>
<tr><td>Name: _______________</td><td>Class: _______________</td></tr>
</table>

All decisions are based upon some basic rules and regulations that we follow every day. If you had the authority to make any three rules that must be followed in your society or country, what would they be? Mention them here.

Rule 1: ____

Reasons:

____

____

____

Rule 2: ____

Reasons:

____

____

____

Rule 3: ____

Reasons:

____

____

____

5.3 COUNTING ON OTHERS FOR HELP

Counting on others means showing confidence in close loved ones to have your back whenever you need them. Every person has a specialized skill that we assign to them, and we are most likely to go to them for that particular skill needs.

It is best to see how your students assign these roles to their loved ones and why they expect them to fill those shoes at any given moment.

Goal: Making small decisions that can improve some aspects of daily life.

Instructions for Teacher:

- Ask the students to mention the names and reasons for people they can always count on in the worksheet provided ahead.
- Discuss in class how they reached this decision and when.

- You can also ask them what they do to make such decisions. Is there a process or any other reason behind their actions?

<table>
<tr><td>Date: _______________</td><td>Day: _______________</td></tr>
<tr><td>Name: _______________</td><td>Class: _______________</td></tr>
</table>

In daily life occurrences, you may need help from others once in a while. The question is who you can trust to support and assist you in your time of need. There are a few situations given below. Answer: who will you ask for help for that particular job and why?

Bike Riding Lessons____

____

Improving One's Performance in a Sport____________________________

____

Gaining Knowledge about Various Subjects___________________________

____

Clearing Snow from the Home Entrance_____________________________

____

Picking out Clothes____

____

Helping With Your Homework________________________________

____

Choosing an Outfit for a Social Event_____________________

____

5.4 WEIGHING OPTIONS BEFORE ACTING

Telling students to have an internal debate before acting on suspicions is one thing that most kids are not willing to try out on their own. If you think that they need some examples to learn thinking before jumping the gun in any situation, try out this activity.

Goal: Teaching the importance of the golden rule: "Think before acting."

Instructions for Teacher:

- Have a class discussion where you make groups of students in fours or fives to research and give a few pointers on why we need to think before jumping to conclusions.
- Let them formulate the reasoning to present to the class in an informal style.
- Then, distribute the worksheet in groups and ask them to fill it out after discussing the given scenarios.

- Have a look at their answers and discuss them with the whole class if they have missed any important factors.

Date: ___________________   Day: ___________________

Name: ___________________   Class: ___________________

It is important to remember that you must think before speaking your thoughts out loud. Look at the scenarios below and answer the questions accordingly.

How does Susan know so? _______________________________________

Is Susan making accusations against David? _______________________

Why would Susan assume David did it? ____________________________

Do you believe Susan thought before speaking? ____________________

How does Matt know Fabian struck him? _________________________

Did he see Fabian hitting him? _________________________

Why did he assume Fabian was responsible? _________________________

What should Matt do? _________________________

5.5 OPTING FOR SMART CHOICES

Teach your students the importance of making smart choices and unconsciously opting to use the pre-made rules that enhance the quality of their lives and choices. It is best to create an environment of accepting the circumstances and being wise in hard moments of life.

Goal: The process of reaching decisions and how they play a role in shaping the future.

Instructions for Teacher:

- Ask the students on how they decide what to do in any given situation.
- Take in their opinions and discuss how each situation has different requirements that are discussed then and there.
- Give out the worksheets to fill out and tell the students to note how each prompt brings many thoughts and how it helps them in reaching a final decision.

- Have a discussion later where students may ask you anything that they may be confused about.

Date: _______________   Day: _______________

Name: _______________   Class: _______________

Please indicate which option(s) you believe would be reasonable in each case by marking them with a check mark. If you can't find a suitable option, make one up yourself and write it in the options.

- At the end of the school day, your school teacher has requested that you arrange the seats on the desks. What do you do?

____ Ask for your friend's help to complete the task quickly.
____ Say "Yes," then forget about it.
____ Start cleaning whiteboards instead.
____ ____

- Your mother is telling you to tidy up your room. What do you do?

____ Have your younger sister clean it for you.
____ Clean it up yourself.
____ Suggest doing it after school to get away.
____ ____

- You watch as a few children steal the lunch box of another kid and run away. What do you do?

____ Do nothing.

____ Chase after the children and see if you can get it.

____ Advise the other kid to do something about it.

____ ________________________________

- Near the playground, you come upon a wallet. What do you do?

____ Go back to your house and hide it

____ Remove the cash from the wallet.

____ Go to the main office of the school and turn in the wallet.

____ ________________________________

5.6 SNAP VS. WELL-THOUGHT OUT DECISIONS

Learning the uses and misuses of making the right decisions at the right time is better. It can be done by giving students time to think about how any situation can be handled in a better way. Give kids authority to make small decisions in class and outside to strengthen their decision-making.

Goal: Discovering the difference between types of decisions and in which situations they can help.

Instructions for Teacher:

- Ask the students to distribute the worksheets and write down their thoughts after discussing these questions amongst themselves:
    - How many types of decisions are there?
    - Is there any reason that makes people tilt to one side?
    - Can you do anything that teaches you to make balanced decisions?

- After 20-30 minutes, ask them to provide unified answers to the questions and turn in their filled worksheets.

Date: _________________ Day: _________________

Name: _______________ Class: _______________

Snap and well-thought-out decisions are opposites. Give a few examples of your decisions that can be categorized as such.

Snap Decisions	Well-Thought Decisions

According to your understanding, answer the given questions:

When should you make snap decisions?

____

____

____

____

When should you make well-thought-out decisions?

____

____

____

____

5.7 My Reasons Behind Decisions

No matter what we do in a day, simply picking up a cup of coffee in the morning or deciding on the biggest decision of our life yet, we are all with a purpose in mind. You cannot make any decision without thinking. Allow your students to check the basis of their decisions.

Goal: Figuring out the main reasons that motivate kids while making big decisions.

Instructions for Teacher:

- When you have discussed why or how decisions are made, ask the students to ponder upon which of their decisions fall in which of the categories of the next worksheet.
- Tell them to think back to anything that comes to their mind for the previous day, week, or two weeks.
- Once done with the worksheets, ask all students to go one-by-one and tell which of their boxes has the most entries and what they believe are the reasons for that.

Consider the previous choices you have made and the motivation behind them. Take note of these choices and record them where they belong.

My choice was based on...

I simply felt like it.	It is something that I always do.
I observed someone else do exactly that.	My teachers or parents told me to do that.
It is my favorite of all.	It was the correct thing to do.

5.8
ACTION CONSEQUENCES!

Actions are always followed by reactions, and kids will learn it soon enough. Why not teach them how their own actions have brought what upon them?

Use this worksheet to help guide your students toward doing actions that are mostly in their or someone else's best interest.

Goal: Learning the consequences of actions through introspection.

Instructions for Teacher:

- Give away the worksheet to students and ask them to fill it according to the instructions provided on it.
- Ask them to share if they gained any insights from solving the worksheet.

Date: ________________   Day: ________________

Name: ________________   Class: ________________

Write down any actions you took today. It could be as simple as deciding to play football during recess to sharing your pencil with a class fellow. Then, answer if that action had any consequences, like playing football making you sleepy and tired after the break.

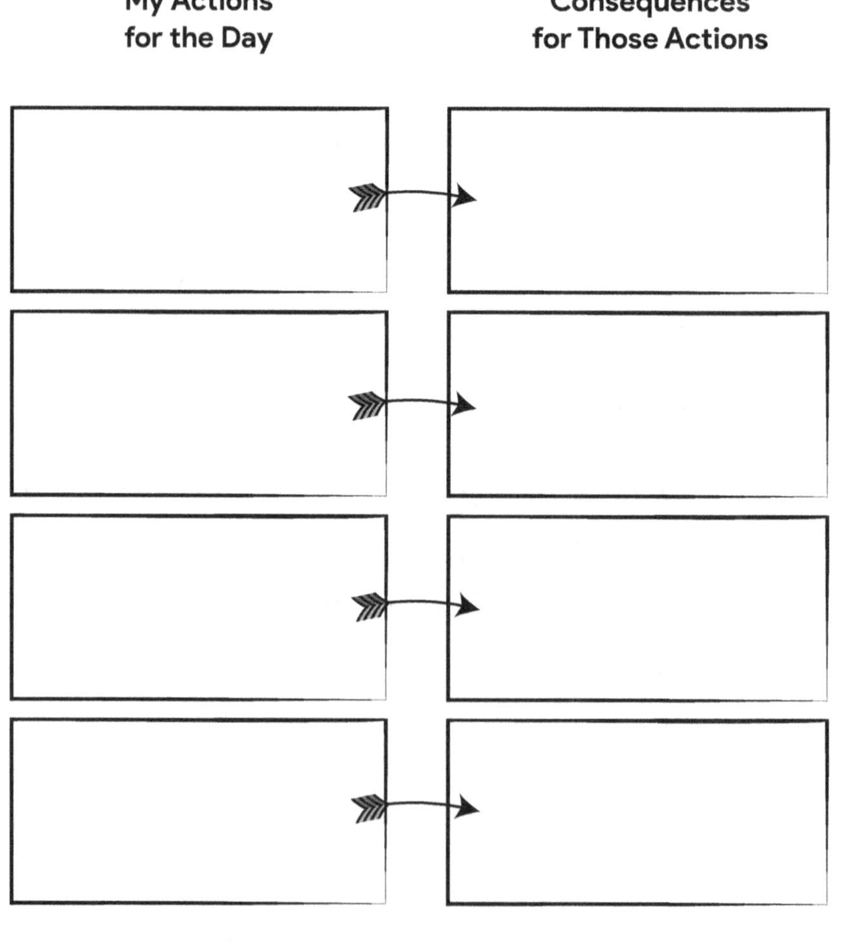

**My Actions
for the Day**

**Consequences
for Those Actions**

5.9
OPPOSING THE NEGATIVE INFLUENCES

Negative influences can be easily thwarted if someone decides to look at the facts of situations and make informed decisions. Teach them to look at all the important factors of situations they find themselves in and find solutions that can help them bring more positive changes in life.

Goal: Fight the negative influences by finding the source of the problem.

Instructions for Teacher:

- Read aloud the scenario given in the worksheet after giving the sheets to the students.
- Have a small discussion to clear any doubts in their mind and tell them to discuss what they have understood from listening/reading it.
- Have them fill out the worksheet and then talk about what they have written down and why.

Read the given scenario and find out the adverse effects of negative influences.

Lily has escaped from her house two times now. Both times, she has gotten herself into a lot of trouble because of her behavior. She even got an ultimatum from her stepfather to call the police next time or send her to live with her father in another state.

After a few consultations with her counselor, Lily has resolved that she will not run away from home again. Instead, she'll find another method to resolve her differences with her mother and stepfather, particularly if they stop nagging her about dating Edward.

Lily has decided that _______________________________

____

____

____

____

____

____

Potential factors that might sway her decision include:

1. _______________________________________

2. _______________________________________

3. _______________________________________

She can resist influences by:

1. _______________________________________

2. _______________________________________

3. _______________________________________

5.10
AFTERMATH OF MY CHOICES

(Best to be paired with activity 5.8)

Having a clear idea in the head often includes the knowledge of planning the present and future consequences before acting on the impulse. If your students are more careful in understanding the positive and negative aspects of their actions, they are more likely to grow into upstanding citizens of the state later.

Goal: Looking at the instant and long-term effects of decisions kids may have faced in their lives.

Instructions for Teacher:

- Give out the worksheets to students.
- Tell them to think more about the consequences of their actions but with long-term future effects in mind.
- Have a discussion later to know the answers and their reasons.

Date: _______________   Day: _______________

Name: _______________   Class: _______________

Our choices have both immediate and lasting consequences. Completing the sections below will help you reflect on how your decisions have impacted you and others.

A choice I made earlier today:

Immediate impact	Potential long-term consequences

A choice I made the day before:

Immediate impact	Potential long-term consequences

A choice I made just last week:

Immediate impact	Potential long-term consequences

5.11 BONUS: BECOMING A LEADER

Leadership can be a quality that makes the most amount of impact on growing kids. They can learn or enhance other skills if they believe they are worthy of becoming a leader one day.

Start by pointing out their best qualities to make them believe in themselves.

Goal: Bringing out qualities of leadership that are present in students.

Instructions for Teacher:

- Ask each student in your class to name one quality in which they excel.
- You and other students may help them find one if they are unsure themselves.
- Then, provide them with available art supplies to make a poster of their leadership quality. It needs to mention why a leader must have that quality to succeed.

- Show them the poster given ahead to use as a muse for their own concepts.

Date: _______________   Day: _______________

Name: _______________   Class: _______________

CONCLUDING THE LEARNING SESSION

Alas, our session has come to an end. I can only hope it has been a fun learning for you and your kids as much as it has been for me writing it. I have always wanted to contribute to society in a bigger way than I have been able to, but I feel this is the right medium to convey the teachings, insights, and everything else that I have learned in my teaching experience.

In my opinion, no teaching style or methodology is without its own merit. It entirely depends on the needs of students, and if you feel that someone needs less conventional support, I say take the leap!

We, educators, cannot take a passive role in our student's life because their future is in our hands to be molded into something uniquely theirs. For that reason, I would urge all my fellow teachers to go with novel approaches and ideas because the world is changing rapidly, and so are the kids.

Take them along for the ride by learning very relevant and revolutionary teachings of SEL that can help them be the builders of their destinies. Help them to help themselves by introducing practical applications of necessary skills that will take them very far in their life.

ABOUT THE AUTHOR

Floriana S. has been a teacher for eight years at the local public middle school in Virginia. She has been a strong advocate of adopting interactive teaching methods in classrooms by incorporating different activities, sessions, workshops, and other things that make kids more interested in learning and becoming something.

Her book "Social-Emotional Learning Activities for Kids" is an effort to bring her hard learned experience to other teachers who are looking for some alternative learning options for their students that teach real life skills in a fun manner.